The
Budget
Entrepreneur™

Starting Your Own Business Without Breaking the Bank

Arthurian Press books are available at special quantity discounts to use as premiums and sales promotions, or for use in corporate training programs. To contact a representative, please visit the Contact Us page at www.arthurianpress.com.

ISBN: 978-0-9962620-0-2

Products, trademarks, and trademarked names are used throughout this book to describe various proprietary products that are owned by third parties. No endorsement of the information contained in this book is given by the owners of such products and trademarks, and no endorsement is implied by the inclusion of products or trademarks in this book.

The **Budget** Entrepreneur™

Starting Your Own Business Without Breaking the Bank

BRIAN ROUEIHEB

ARTHURIAN
PRESS

A Division of Arthurian Enterprises

Contents

Introduction

For millions of Americans the American dream doesn't just include a home with a white picket fence; it also includes being their own boss, and running a business enterprise of their own. Many with this same dream may be under the impression that starting a new business is overly complicated or expensive. This may lead them to believe that although they think they've got a great idea, they should hold off on acting on it until they've got more time and/or money to see it through.

The truth is that there's no reason to wait. It might surprise you just how simple and affordable starting your own business can be. If you're on a tight budget you likely won't be able to quit your day job overnight. However, if you've got an idea and the drive to see it through, there's no reason you couldn't or shouldn't start your dream business enterprise on a smaller scale.

I got my first job at the age of 15, working part time as a graphic designer at a local copy shop. I soon discovered that I had my own ideas for offering local businesses better and more expansive design services. As soon as I graduated I opened my first side business, offering graphic and web design services beyond what was offered at what had by then become my full-time job. Today, I run a small marketing and consulting firm in Southern California that I founded 12 years ago. Through my firm I've counseled countless small businesses through the startup process. Many of which have gone on to continue working with my firm to successfully craft and market their brands.

I was recently sitting with a new client who I had just guided through the process of starting his first business. He told me that if he had known it was this easy to start his own business he would have done it years ago. He was so amazed at how quickly and affordably he was able to get his business setup with my guidance, that he half-jokingly suggested that I should write a book on the subject. I chuckled at the thought initially, but the more I thought about it the more I realized that there probably were others that could benefit from my knowledge and experiences in starting a business, and so here we are…

When you're starting a new business you're going to want to spend whatever hard earned money you've got on the things you need to run your business, like marketing and raw materials. No one wants to blow through their startup money just getting the business formed. Throughout this book I'm going to share with you the tips and tricks I've learned and taught to others over the years on how to get up and running without breaking the bank.

Of course there are many books on the subject of starting your own business, but most seem to spend more time on business fundamentals and planning than anything else. I'm going to touch on some of this information briefly, and then jump right into the actual meat of the subject. The fundamentals of business and how to write a business plan have been covered before. This book is meant to be more of a practical guide through the steps necessary in starting a business, rather than an introduction to economics, or a book on how to write a business plan.

I'll begin this book by urging you to do your due diligence. I'll recommend you of course write up a business plan, but I'll insist that you at least devise a mission statement and do some basic market research before really getting started. You will then be presented with a basic rundown of the different business entity types that are most commonly used for small businesses. Forming your desired entity type will be covered, along with the fictitious business name process, and how to make sure you're operating in accordance with local law.

Throughout this book I'll be pointing out some common and potentially costly pit falls to avoid along the way. I'll also be sharing some of my own personal experiences and recommendations while covering topics that include establishing banking, merchant services, workspace, and more. By the end of this short book, I'll have covered just about everything you'll need to know on how to get into business for yourself, without having to drain your checkbook in the process! The book will end with presenting some ideas on what your next steps might be, once your business hits its stride and becomes profitable.

The Budget Entrepreneur

Chapter 1
Before You Start(up)

As anyone will advise you, the first thing you *should* do before starting a business is put together a solid business plan. This is absolutely sound advice. A good business plan will, among other things: layout your company's mission, calculate the required opening and operating expenses, and present marketing research that should show the business can be profitable. A good business plan will also spell out the company's initial and long-term goals along with the steps needed to reach them. Having this information put together will help you stay on budget and focused on what needs to be accomplished to take your business from startup to profit. I'm not going to delve further into the how and why of creating a business plan. The fact of the matter is that this particular subject deserves a book in itself, and I'm sure there are several of such books available out there.

While it is ideal to know exactly what you're getting into, and to have the needed cash flow in reserve to cover your first several months of operation; the most important thing is that you have an idea and the drive to take that idea to market. According to the 2008 US economic census there are some 27 million companies in the US. A whopping 21 million of which are businesses with no employees. These are self-employed individuals aspiring for entrepreneurial success just like you. Out of 21 million small businesses, it's safe to assume that a great deal of them likely got started without the best of planning or optimal initial funding. If you've got a good idea and the drive to execute it, there's no reason why you can't or shouldn't get started on a smaller scale with a tight budget, and I'm going to teach you how to do just that.

I'm in no way saying that you shouldn't have a business plan in place or that you shouldn't save up enough money to comfortably launch your business. You should have a thorough business plan written up before opening a business, you should see a certified tax professional before selecting a business entity, and you should of course have enough money in reserve to cover all of your operating expenses for at least the first several months of operation. That being said; a lot of people simply don't have the means to do all these things. I, for one, don't think there is any reason that such a person should let their financial situation, or lack of ability to put together a professional business plan, discourage them from trying to start their own business.

I started my first business fresh out of high school and had no clue what I was doing at the time. I also didn't have more than a hundred dollars to my name. While that first business ultimately didn't work out, the lessons I learned in the process of figuring out what it took to start a business were invaluable to me in my future endeavors. This book will touch upon some legal and tax related aspects of starting a business, and perhaps present some information meant to help you in making the decisions you'll be faced with along the way. It is, however, important to keep in mind that the information provided does not constitute the legal or accounting advice of a licensed professional. In case you need such advice, be sure to consult with an appropriately licensed attorney or tax professional.

If you haven't put together a full-fledged business plan, it is still important that you at the very least take the time to complete two fundamental parts of any good business plan before proceeding.

The first part is to create a mission statement for your business. This fundamental part of any business plan is in fact the foundation of your business itself. A mission statement is usually just a few short sentences in length. It essentially spells out what exactly the company is setting out to accomplish, and the philosophies that will be practiced in the process.

Here are two examples of what a mission statement might look like, from two different non-existent companies:

XYZ Enterprises is a company devoted to bringing affordable solar power solutions to the residential market. We motivate and encourage homeowners to make the switch to clean energy. We believe that together, we can make our future greener.

ABC Catering is a spunky, imaginative catering company aimed at offering high-quality, affordably priced, occasionally unconventional meals using only the freshest natural ingredients. Our goals are simple: making great food, annual profitability, and promoting sustainable local farms.

The mission statement summarizes for your community, vendors, customers, and employees, what the purpose of your company's existence is and what your company's core values are. This is important because moving forward you and your future employees will want to first consider the company's mission statement before making any important strategic decisions. This will ensure that the decisions made within your organization are done in accordance with and in support of your company's brand, ethics, and goals.

The second part is to conduct some basic research on the market your business will be operating within. I can't emphasize enough how important this is. In my line of work I get pitched new business and product ideas all the time. The worst part of what I do is having to tell someone with an idea they're passionate about (who hasn't done this basic research), that they just don't have a realistic chance of success in their marketplace. No one wants to hear that their business idea is doomed to failure after they've already invested time and money into it. The worst thing you could do is put yourself in that position. An estimated 50% of all small businesses fail within their first year. This, in my experience, can often be attributed to a lack of adequate market research being done by business owners before starting their businesses. I can't stress enough how important it is to take the relatively small amount of time it will take you to do this research.

You'll first want to determine the market and market area your business will be targeting. If you were opening a local graphic design firm you would likely be researching the graphic design market in your local geographic area. If you were going to start building your own brand of bicycles and selling them online you would likely be researching the bicycle market on the Internet. You would start by researching the competition within your market area. You'll want to gauge their pricing, products/services, customer service, and perceived reputation and position within the market.

What you are trying to do in all of this is gauge what your competition's strengths and weaknesses are, and compare them to your own. You want to make sure that you have the resources and ability to compete with your competition before you begin spending money starting the business up. This can potentially save a lot of time and money if your research happens to show that you will be unable to competitive in the marketplace.

I'm going to proceed to describe how you might conduct some basic market research using each of the two sample business models mentioned earlier. This way regardless of whether your business is going to be product or service based, or whether it will sell within a specific geographic area or online, you'll be able to see what things you should be looking for.

If you were starting a graphic design firm that serviced clients in San Diego for example, you would start by identifying what other businesses provide graphic design services in that same area. With that list you would then check out their websites, their advertising, any reviews you could find, and any pricing you could get your hands on. Ideally you would find that you can be competitive with your strongest competition on all fronts. This would mean that your business idea is lucrative and there's no reason not to move forward. If however you were to find that you can match their Internet presence and even one up their marketing efforts, but can't afford to price your services competitively to theirs, you may have want to take pause to do some further research. You might do some more searching online and find them on a business review site like Yelp (http://www.yelp.com). If they have numerous reviews averaging one and a half stars then perhaps you could still find success by offering a higher level of a service at an albeit slightly higher price. If they happened to have numerous reviews averaging five stars, you might instead decide its time to start looking at other ideas before further committing to what would appear to be an uphill battle.

If instead you were opening a company making your own brand of high-end bicycles that you planned on selling online, you would start by identifying who else was selling high-end bicycles of similar style and build quality online. You would want to thoroughly go through their websites to gauge their design and find more information on their bicycles. You would also want to find out how they're advertising, and track down all the reviews you could find on retail sites and bicycle enthusiast forums. You'd also want to scour the Internet to find the lowest retail price these competing bicycles can be purchased for. Ideally you would find that you can sell a higher quality bicycle at a lower price, and can create a website and marketing strategy just as good if not better than your strongest competition. This would mean that the business idea is lucrative and there's no reason not to move forward. If however you were to find that you're proposed bicycles use higher grade materials requiring them to be sold at a higher price than competing bicycles, you might consider holding off on moving forward until you can dig a little deeper. In this case you might start posting on numerous bicycle enthusiast sites and forums to share your concepts and verify interest in the marketplace for a higher-end bicycle sold at a higher selling point. If you got an overwhelmingly positive response you might consider moving forward. If you faced resistance or lack of response, you might instead want to look at making some changes to your business model or start looking at other ideas before committing to starting a business that there doesn't appear to be a demand for.

Unfortunately, some people will inevitably find out that their 'great idea' just isn't going to cut it in the current market. Perhaps they have an original product idea but they find someone else already invented and patented it. Maybe their plan to make widgets gets hampered when they find they can't make and sell them as cheap as their competition. Whatever the reason, should this happen to you, don't be discouraged. You don't have to discard your dream of running your own business. You merely need to adjust it. Figure out how to innovate within your proposed market in a way that your competition currently isn't, or try to think of another market or niche that you think you can innovate and compete within.

Chapter 2
Choosing a Business Entity Type

The first step in actually forming your new business is going to be deciding on the type of business entity it will be. Your chosen business entity type ultimately determines the business structure of the company, as well as how it will be taxed. In the United States, the most common entity types formed by small businesses are: corporations (most commonly Subchapter C or S corporations), partnerships, LLCs, and sole proprietorships.

Let's take a brief look at these different types of entities so you can determine which one is best suited for your business. Spoiler Alert: There's a 70% chance that the right entity for your small business is a sole proprietorship, but more on that later.

Corporations

Corporations are treated as legal entities separate from their owner(s). Subchapter C corporations are also going to be treated as a separate entity for tax purposes as well. As such 'C' corporations are responsible for filing annual tax returns. Subchapter S corporations are different in that while still treated as separate legal entities, their profits and losses are directly passed through to their owners for the sake of taxation. This ability to essentially avoid 'double taxation' may or may not prove beneficial for some smaller businesses. By 'double taxation' I mean a corporation being initially taxed on its income, and then its owner(s) being additionally taxed on any dividends or salary received from the corporation. Because corporations are considered separate legal entities from their owners, this business structure will usually limit the owner's personal liability in the company to some extent. This means that creditors or anyone taking legal action against a corporation will generally not be able to pursue action against the owner(s), except of course in cases involving fraud. This may be an important deciding factor to businesses that have a high risk of liability or in situations where the owners have personal assets they need to protect.

Corporations can be owned by one or more people and even other corporations. The equity stake of the owners in a corporation is called the corporation's 'stock' or 'capital stock'. A corporation will declare how many shares make up the company's stock when initially formed, and those shares can then be distributed to the owner(s) to determine percentage of ownership. For example, if XYZ Incorporated was comprised of 10,000 shares of stock and had one owner, that owner would be issued all 10,000 shares to show 100% ownership. If later that owner wanted to add on an investor as a 25% equity partner/owner he would simply sell 2,500 shares to the new co-owner.

This ease in transferring ownership, and possible liability protection, doesn't come without a price however. Corporations are required to keep up on more paperwork such as creating bylaws, keeping minutes, filing annual reports with the state, obtaining an EIN (employer identification number), etc. Please keep in mind that you should check your Secretary of State's website for information on the costs of forming and maintaining this type of entity in your state.

Going forward I'm going to reference some of the costs for fees found in California to provide an idea of the potential expenditure involved with maintaining a corporate entity. Besides the state fees you'll be charged to form the corporation ($100 in California for example), filing your annual reports with the state is going to almost always cost you a few dollars ($20 in California) annually. You may also be liable for other annual taxation or fees. In California, for example, there is a minimum franchise tax on corporations of $800, regardless of if the company made profit or not. This is all in addition to any fees for the business license your corporation will also need to obtain at the city or county level in order to operate. Because of the extra paperwork, formal procedure, and costs required, corporations are generally best left to businesses whose owners need to try and limit their liability, or have already grown large enough to be able to handle the associated responsibilities and fees required to maintain a corporate entity without batting an eye. Otherwise the costs, formal procedures, and increased paperwork involved in maintaining this type of entity may quickly overwhelm small businesses on a tight budget. It is probably also worth noting that owners of a corporation can't just pay out profits to themselves in the form of dividends. Corporations must first pay a 'reasonable' salary, with all the taxes and bookkeeping that entails, to any owners that are involved in the operation of the business before any dividends can be disbursed.

Corporations are formed by drafting a document called 'articles of incorporation' and filing it with your Secretary of State's office. The articles of incorporation act as a charter to establish your business. This document must set forth certain information that will vary from state to state. In general the document will outline the company's name, address, agent for service of process, and the amount and type of stock being issued. You'll also be expected to draft a document called 'by-laws' for your corporation. Corporate by-laws act as the operational blueprint of a corporation. The by-laws establish the rights, powers, and responsibilities of the shareholders, directors, and officers. If you were dead set on starting your business as a corporation, the most economic route to go is to search online for some general templates for your articles of incorporation and by-laws. You would then customize them for your new company, making sure they comply with any applicable state requirements, and then file the articles of incorporation with the state yourself. After that, you need only obtain an EIN (employer identification number) before you can proceed to get a local business license and open a bank account. EIN numbers are issued by the IRS and can in many cases by easily obtained through the IRS website (http://www.irs.gov/Businesses/) at no cost. This is easier then it sounds and you can save hundreds of dollars by doing this all yourself.

There are numerous companies you may come across online that offer to 'affordably' incorporate your business in your state for you. These companies do little more than use the same freely available document templates for the required documentation, pocketing hundreds of dollars for essentially doing nothing. Whether you do it yourself, or choose to use one of these services to help you incorporate, you need to understand that if your corporate documents are not properly drafted for your organization you may find that that your entity gets thrown aside if the company is ever challenged in court. This would result in any liability falling on the owner(s), essentially nullifying the whole purpose of even starting a corporation. So if you really want to start a corporation you should speak with a licensed attorney for help drafting these important documents first. This of course will cost you, but if you've got the assets to protect, then you have the money to spend; if you don't then this probably isn't the entity type for you anyway.

Partnerships

Partnerships are a business entity type owned by two or more people. Partnerships are not considered separate entities from their owners and so all liability, profit, and loss are passed through to the owners. For tax purposes this works by splitting up the profit and loss between owners according to their percentage of ownership. For example, lets assume a partnership of two people accumulates $100,000 in profit and $40,000 in debt over the calendar year. If both owners are equal partners, they both claim $50,000 of the profit and $20,000 of the debt on their personal taxes. If the same company's ownership was split 75% and 25%: the majority owner would claim $75,000 of the profit and $30,000 of the debt, while the minority partner would claim $25,000 of the profit and $10,000 of the debt on their personal taxes. In this fashion the liability of the company is also split amongst the owners.

General partnerships usually won't require filing any paperwork with the state in addition to obtaining a business license at the city or county level like every other type of business entity. Partnerships do however require obtaining an EIN from the IRS. This number is used to annually report the profits and losses of the business to the IRS, although partnerships are not taxed directly by the IRS like a Subchapter C corporation would be. This information is merely reported so that it can be reconciled with the information provided on the owners' tax returns.

It is strongly recommended that you do not enter a partnership without a properly written partnership agreement, or 'articles of partnership', protecting all involved parties. Because all partners in a partnership share in the profit and loss of the company it is important to have an agreement in place that spells out the roles of each partner. If there is an even number of partners it is also important this document defines how decisions are to be made if the opinion amongst the owners is evenly split.

A general partnership is essentially a sole proprietorship that happens to be owned by more than one person. Like a sole proprietorship, there are minimal entity-related bookkeeping and procedural requirements (annual state filings, holding annual meetings and recording the minutes, etc.), and as the entity is not considered separate from the owners there is generally no liability protection.

Limited Liability Companies (LLCs)

Limited liability companies are a newer entity type. It may be easiest to think of them as the offspring of the corporation and partnership, or perhaps more simply a cousin of the Subchapter S corporation. LLCs can be formed by one or more individuals, and are considered separate legal entities from their owner(s), just like a corporation. The profit and loss of an LLC is generally passed directly through to the owner(s) like an S corporation or partnership. An LLC is however unique in that you can choose how it gets taxed. This means that if you wanted for whatever reason to open an LLC and have it be taxed like a Subchapter C corporation, you could. LLCs are also required to obtain an EIN from the IRS. LLCs are usually formed by filing 'articles of organization' with the your Secretary of State. This document is very similar to the 'articles of incorporation' that would be used to charter a corporation. Filing this document with your state is usually done at a fee ($70 in California). An LLC will also need to obtain a business license at the city or county level just like every other entity type.

As the name implies, owner liability of this entity type is limited in much the same way it would be in a corporation. LLCs may also be subject to the same additional annual state fees and taxes as corporations. In California, for example, the minimum $800 franchise tax applies to corporations and LLCs alike. An LLC is essentially very similar to an S corporation, except with more relaxed entity-related bookkeeping and procedural requirements similar to that of a partnership. As with starting a corporation you should definitely speak with a tax professional or attorney for help determining if this entity structure is right for you, and making sure all your required documentation is in order. This will of course cost you, but as I've said before, if you've got the assets to protect then you have the money to spend; if you don't then this probably isn't the entity type for you anyway.

Sole Proprietorships

Sole proprietorships are the meat and potatoes of the small business world. In fact, over 70 percent of all small businesses are sole proprietorships according to the SBA (Small Business Association). This is most likely because sole proprietorships are the simplest and least expensive type of business entity to establish. There is generally no registration or annual filing required at the state level. You'll essentially just need to obtain a business license at the local city or county level, like any other entity type. A sole proprietorship is not considered a separate entity from the owner. This means that all the profit, loss, and liability of the business is passed through to the owner. The profit and loss are reported on the owner's personal income taxes by submitting a Schedule C form in conjunction with the standard Form 1040 to the IRS at tax time.

Having no built-in liability protection may seem scary to some. However, I look at it this way: If you don't have the money to spend on paying a professional to help you establish an LLC or corporation, then you've likely got nothing to lose anyway. If you do have the money to spend on hiring a professional to help you form an LLC or corporation, and maintaining one of these entity types, then you probably have assets worth protecting. In this case you should certainly pay a professional to help you establish an LLC or corporation to protect your assets. However, if you are starting out on a budget you'll most likely be forming a sole proprietorship. When your company starts making you enough money that it makes sense to protect your new assets from liability, you can simply incorporate (or organize an LLC) at that point.

You may have noticed that the other entity types described so far have required that an EIN number be acquired at the time of formation. Since a sole proprietorship is not considered a separate entity from the owner, the owner's social security number is used as the business's tax identification number. This means an EIN will only be required if and when the sole proprietorship ever hires employees. This is in fact the very purpose of the EIN: providing a number and means for the IRS to track withholding taxes owed on employees.

Chapter 3
A Rose by Any Other Name (Requires a DBA)

For those of you following along, by now you should have put together a business plan (or at least have defined a clear mission statement, and have researched your intended market to verify you can be successful within it). You also likely decided on the entity type you will form your new business into. If you are one of the few new businesses starting up as a partnership, LLC, or corporation: you may have already filed the appropriate filings with the state and obtained an EIN from the IRS as well.

For LLCs and Corporations, this process will have already included naming your entity following some basic guidelines that vary slightly from state to state. You are essentially free to create the fictitious business name of your choosing at the time of formation for these entity types, provided that the 'root' business name is unique within the state you are operating in, and that you attach the appropriate suffix at the end of the business name. The proposed business name must also not be misleading, or too similar to an existing business name. For LLCs the appropriate suffix to attach at the end of the business name would generally be one of the following: LLC, L.L.C., Limited Liability Company, or Limited Company. For corporations the appropriate suffix to attach to the end of the business name would generally be: Incorporated, Corporation, Inc., or Corp. Earlier I mentioned earlier that the 'root' business name must be unique. This means that aside from not being allowed to form 'Acme Corporation' if another 'Acme Corporation' exists within your state, you also couldn't form 'Acme Corporation' if there was already an 'Acme LLC'.

For sole proprietorships the business name is by default the legal name of the owner. In the case of partnerships, the legal business name is by default the combined legal names of all the partners. This is obviously less than desirable in most cases, and you may very likely want to give your business a more suitable name to conduct business as. Even if you had started an LLC or corporation, you may still want to conduct business under a different name then the business's original legal name you gave it at formation.

You can call your business by another name by registering a fictitious business name (FBN), which is sometimes also known as a DBA (doing business as). The process and fees for this vary from jurisdiction to jurisdiction, but generally you'll register a DBA by visiting the county clerk office in your county (as is the case in California; in New Jersey for example this is actually handled at the state level). Most of the time the fee for registering a fictitious business name is going to vary from $30 to $60, but again this will vary from one jurisdiction to the next. The forms involved are relatively simple and straightforward. Following registration most jurisdictions are going to also require publication. The rules on this will again vary slightly from area to area, but generally it will be required that you publish a 'fictitious business name statement' for four consecutive weeks in a court approved local publication. It is usually required that the first publication date be within 30 days of the fictitious business name's registration.

Publication is one area in particular that you can lose a lot of money if you aren't savvy. I can't speak to all jurisdictions, but in Southern California for example, at any given county clerk's office there will be no less then 10 solicitors huddling around the entrances, and even lurking around the halls, trying to sucker you into paying way too much for a publication before you have the chance to even register your fictitious business name. Just the other day I took an old friend of mine to one of the county clerk's offices in Los Angeles, to walk him through getting his first DBA. As we were walking in we noticed a young man get hooked by a solicitor right in front of us. The solicitor then proceeded to follow the young man around the courthouse, through a 15-minute wait in line, and then proceeded to stand right over his shoulder while he registered his name with a clerk. He did all this just to make sure this poor sap wouldn't escape without being suckered into paying too much for his FBN publication.

Unfortunately, people fall for these solicitors' slick talk and persistency in this fashion all the time. This is of course obviously why the solicitors keep at it. However, you aren't just at risk of paying too much by giving these solicitors your business, you're also at risk of not getting published at all! If some guy just walks up to you and says he's with a newspaper, you have virtually no way of verifying that on the spot. So many times people are simply handing over cash to scam artists and end up paying double in the long run, for what should in reality be one of the simplest standard procedures in starting a business.

What you'll want to do is visit your county clerk's website (or the website of whatever agency in your jurisdiction grants FBNs), because they'll list the publication requirements and all the court approved publications within that jurisdiction that you can publish your fictitious business name statement in. From there you'll want to visit the websites of these publications, or call if need be, to find the best bargain in your area. A hint here would be to check the most obscure sounding publications first.

Obviously a major paper will charge an arm and a leg to publish these sorts of notices in it, but a smaller neighborhood specific weekly publication that is also approved for fictitious business name statement publication by the court will often prove to be a much less expensive alternative. Again using Southern California as an example, solicitors outside the county clerk's office will try to drain you for $80 to $120 for a publication. Whereas if you spent a few minutes searching online you'd find you could publish an Orange County FBN in the "Mission Viejo News", who will publish an FBN statement for just $22, which includes providing you with proof of publication (more on this in a bit) and filing the county required 'proof of publication affidavit' with the county clerk.

In Los Angeles county a little searching online will yield that the 'British Weekly' will publish your FBN statement for just $30, which also includes the proof of publication and filing of the 'proof of publication affidavit' with the county clerk. The proof of publication that you receive from these publications will often be required to be shown along with other paperwork to the bank when opening your business checking account (so be sure not to lose it).

Chapter 4
Licensing, the Final Frontier

The final step in establishing your company is going to be obtaining a business license, and any other licenses or permits that may be required to lawfully operate in your jurisdiction.

To start with, you'll most likely need a business license from the city or county your business will be operating in. More often than not this business license will be issued at the city level, but this isn't always the case. For example, if you live in an unincorporated city or an unincorporated part of a county, you will likely need to obtain a business license from the county itself.

The business license fees required will either be a flat annual fee, or vary based on income essentially acting as a tax. Lets assume for example that you were opening your small business in the city of Orange, CA. You could then expect to pay about $100 up front and about $100 a year until making over a certain amount of annual sales.

If your business resides in a state that charges sales tax, you'll likely also need to obtain a seller permit from the state. For example, in the county of Orange in California (in which you may have guessed that the city of Orange resides), sales tax is about 8%. So if that same business that you just paid $100 to officially open in the city of Orange happened to plan on selling widgets, you'd have to also go down to the nearest office of the California Board of Equalization to obtain a seller's permit. This (in California at least) would likely not cost anything up front, but your business will be instructed to report on it's income either quarterly or annually, at which time it will be expected to pay the 8% sales tax it was responsible for collecting from its customers when they buy the widgets. This same permit will usually be required to be shown/forwarded to any vendors within the same jurisdiction, to prove your exemption from being charged sales tax for the goods that you make your widgets out of (as your customers will be charged the sales tax on the final product).

If you were solely in the business of providing services, and provided or sold absolutely no physical or tangible goods to your customers, then you would generally not have to obtain a seller's permit or collect sales tax. For example, a business that solely offered consulting services, where all it did was get paid to give verbal advice to it's customers, would likely be exempt from charging or collecting sales tax. If you think your business may be exempt, then you'll want to double check with a certified tax professional in your area to be sure. It probably won't cost much to make a 15-minute appointment just to check if you should be charging sales tax (and will therefore need a seller's permit), and it could save you some time and money in the long run if it turns out that you don't.

Finally, depending on the business your company will be conducting, it may require any number of additional licenses and/or permits. For example there are usually special licenses and permits required for businesses that sell alcohol or tobacco, provides taxi or limo services, prepare food, or operate as a pawnshop, among other things. Most businesses won't be involved with products or services that the government has determined they need to place further controls over. If, however, you have any question that your business may require any additional permits or licenses its definitely better to look into it now rather than potentially risk being penalized down the road for not having the proper licenses and/or permits in order.

The SBA (Small Business Association) actually has a few pages of their site designed to point you to the appropriate federal and local government agencies that you should check with to see what permits or licenses might be required for your particular business:

https://www.sba.gov/content/what-federal-licenses-and-permits-does-your-business-need

https://www.sba.gov/content/what-state-licenses-and-permits-does-your-business-need

You started with a good idea. You then devised a plan, or at least put together a clear mission statement and researched the market to make sure that your idea was profitable. You chose the entity best suited for your new business to initially form into, and filed any applicable paperwork for it. You obtained a fictitious business name if needed, and just got all your required licenses and permits in order. Congratulations, you're officially in business!

The Budget Entrepreneur

Chapter 5

Bargain Business Banking

The first step for any business that has just started up is to establish its business checking account. After all, you're going to need somewhere to keep all the money you're about to make! A business checking account at the average bank is going to end up costing upwards of $15 a month. At the low end that's for a bare bones checking account, which is nothing more than a place to store money and a means of accepting checks. If you want to also be able to take credit cards, you'll also need a merchant account. Most merchant accounts will have some sort of associated minimum monthly fee upwards of $30 a month, in addition to the fees charged per transaction.

Lets start off with business checking. It is going to pay to do some research before choosing a bank. In many instances it may be possible to forgo the need to pay a monthly fee at all if you can find a bank that offers free business checking. This is certainly an oddity in this day and age, but these banks are out there! For example, in Southern California there are a few First Citizen Banks scattered about, and they happen to offer free business checking to businesses that do a relatively small number of transactions a month. There are also more and more online-based banks, that are FDIC insured just like the brick and mortar banks in your area, but that offer free business checking accounts.

It may seem inconvenient to not have a physical branch right around the corner to be able to walk into and do your banking, but with the ability to withdraw cash (if needed) from any ATM, and to make check deposits through these banks' smart phone apps, you might not even feel the difference at all nowadays. There are even websites available where you can enter your estimated banking needs (how much cash you estimate you'll be depositing a month, how many transactions you estimate doing, what your estimated minimum daily balance will be, etc.) and find the banks servicing your area that are best suited to your needs. Often there will be a few free and low cost options to choose from. For example, I usually recommend small business owners check out NerdWallet (http://www.nerdwallet.com/business-checking-accounts/), which comprehensively compares both local and online banks that provide business checking accounts in your area, based on your business's estimated banking needs.

Opening a business checking account, aside from whatever monthly fees might come into play, will of course require a minimum deposit just as most personal checking accounts do. This will usually be $100, although you may find a larger initial deposit may be required at some of the banks offering free checking accounts. You'll also likely need to show your business's paperwork. This will most often include: any filings you've made with the state (articles of incorporation, etc), your EIN if applicable, your business license, as well as your fictitious business name paperwork and corresponding proof of publication.

Once you've opened your business checking account you'll likely next be looking to acquire a means of charging credit cards. Most banks offer merchant services, but again this will easily cost upwards of $30 a month to maintain when you go that route. I instead ordinarily recommend small businesses on a budget start with one of the few merchant service providers that charge no monthly fees outside of the standard per transaction fees. You can always switch to a full-fledged merchant account when you've got the steady sales volume to easily cover the monthly fees involved with one. As a business just starting out on a tight budget: if you can save the $15 a month in banking fees and $30 a month in merchant fees, that $45 a month in savings adds up quick, and will save you hundreds of dollars over the course of the year!

As far as companies that offer merchant services allowing you to accept credit card payment without charging you a minimum monthly fee, there are several options: PayPal, Square, 2Checkout, and Stripe.

If you are going to operate a website that will accept payments for products and/or services through it and want to get setup as easily as possible, you'll want to take a look at opening an account for your new business with PayPal (http://www.PayPal.com). PayPal offers several free and secure options for accepting credit cards online that won't cost you a dime, other than the standard per transaction fee. If, however, you want a more seamless and professional looking checkout process, you'll want to look at alternatives like 2Checkout (http://www.2Checkout.com), or Stripe (http://www.Stripe.com). These companies also offer monthly fee-free merchant services, but will often require more technical knowledge to integrate into your website.

If your business is instead going to be charging credit cards in person, you'll probably want to take a look at Square (http://www.SquareUp.com). Square provides a credit card swiping device that works with most smart phones, and will allow you to swipe cards in person as well as manually enter card information for orders taken over the phone. It should be noted that PayPal also now offers a credit card swiping device for smart phones, but if you are only taking cards in-person Square's service offering seems to be a little more polished in this respect.

If you needed to both accept online payments, and swipe cards in person, you could of course sign up for any combination of these services. All of the services mentioned charge no month fees (at least for their base offerings), and instead usually just charge a slightly higher per transaction fee than you might find with a traditional merchant account. For smaller businesses this trade off will often work in their favor, and you can again always get a full-fledged merchant account whenever you outgrow these services.

Chapter 6

Frugal Workspace

If the business you are entering is going to require that you have space for you to get work done and/or meet with clients at, you might have already browsed through the classifieds for commercial space for rent and cringed at the price of office space these days. You could start off by getting your work done at home, and you could meet your clients at a coffee shop while you're getting on your feet, but these are temporary solutions at best. Personally, in regards to working from home at least, I find there are simply too many distractions that prohibit productivity.

There's a great concept being rolled out all over the country called 'shared workspaces'. These are essentially large offices, with open workspaces and tabletops that provide members with Internet connectivity. For a fee that is usually a fraction of renting even the smallest of offices, you can usually get 24-hour access to one of these facilities where you can sit at any open workspace and get work done in an office environment teeming with other budding entrepreneurs starting out just like you.

Many office buildings will also have a large collection of offices on one of the floors set up as 'Executive Suites' or 'Executive Office Suites'. For the most part, they rent individual offices with reception services at a premium price tag, but many of them will also offer 'virtual office packages'. These packages will allow you to use their business address as your own for your mailing needs, and usually will include, or have the option to add-on a certain amount of hours or days a month usage of a private office or conference room. This can be convenient if you mainly need a professional mailing address and a place to meet clients on occasion.

If and when you are ready to lease dedicated office space for your business, you can always look through classifieds in your local paper, and check through free online classified sites like Craigslist (http://www.craigslist.org) for deals on local commercial space for lease or rent. Sometimes you can even find listings for companies that are renting out spare offices or space within their buildings, often times for much less than you'd pay leasing the same square footage traditionally. If you can afford to be patient, some really great deals on office space can be found every so often.

Chapter 7
Protecting Your Intellectual Property

When you have something of value, you naturally want to protect it. It's easy to think about this in terms of money, cars, and real estate. The truth is there is value to intellectual property as well. If you came up with an amazing name, logo, invention, or design that is totally unique, you'll probably want to protect it so that others can't legally use your intellectual property without your permission.

Names and logos can be protected by 'trademarks', while inventions and designs can be protected by 'patents'. Both are granted by the USPTO (United States Patent & Trademark Office – http://www.uspto.gov). This is unfortunately one area of business where there is just not a lot of money to be saved. The truth is that this is for the most part, a fairly costly process (more so for patents than trademarks). This is because in most situations a patent/trademark attorney will unavoidably be needed to guide you through the process.

With regard to trademarks, if you were absolutely sure that the trademark (name, logo, etc) being registered is unique and unlike anything registered before it, you could potentially save a little bit of money by registering it through one of several online services offering to help walk you through the process for several hundred dollars. However, be forewarned that if there are any issues and the USPTO rejects your claim, you'll likely need to hire an attorney to help you anyway, which may end up costing you more than having seen an attorney in the first place.

There is another much cheaper trademark option however. Registering your trademark with the USPTO allows you to use the registered trademark (®) symbol alongside your name, logo, or mark. However, you are free to claim trademark ownership of any unique name or logo you create using the standard trademark (™) symbol. As long as you keep clear documentation or proof of when you started using the mark in question, this can still help you protect your trademark in court should the need arise. This just doesn't happen to provide as strong of protection as an officially registered trademark. It's a good place to start though, if you don't have the money to register your trademark right away.

When it comes to patents, or protecting inventions and designs, there is simply no way to get around having to hire a patent attorney. The patent process will almost undoubtedly require some amount of back and forth between your attorney and the USPTO, as its highly unlikely that the USPTO will grant a new patent based on the initially submitted application. Usually the USPTO will find one reason or another to reject some or all of your patent application's claims. This will require you to go back and have your attorney draft up a response that narrows or clarifies the scope of your patent in order to hopefully work around the patent examiner's objections. In the best case scenario, which again I've never seen personally, your patent is granted based on the initial application and will end up costing you approximately $3,500 to $4,500. If as in most cases, your patent is initially rejected however, the process will additionally cost approximately $3000 more for every round of office action responses that you need to file. It's not uncommon for the patent process to go back and forth in this fashion several times, and ending up easily costing $12,000 to $20,000 before the patent ever gets granted.

While there's really no way around these costs, if your idea is valuable enough that you think others will try to steal it, these costs are well justified. The process for obtaining a registered trademark can sometimes be completed within just a few months. The process for obtaining a patent takes considerably longer. It's common that a patent will ultimately take years before being granted. That is why you'll commonly see companies talking about their 'patent-pending' inventions or designs. This means they've begun the patent process, but their application is still working its way through the USPTO process.

The Budget Entrepreneur

Chapter 8
Making Sales on a Budget

With your company established, and banking in place, you're ready to start making money! Starting out on a budget the key to growing your business is going to be getting your company, and its products or services, in front of as many people as possible, for as little money as possible. There are a few ways to approach this depending on whether your business is geared toward selling to consumers or towards selling to other businesses.

If your in the business of selling products or services to consumers, you'll want to take a look at ways to get the most public exposure for the least cost. Of course the Internet might immediately come to mind as a convenient and low cost way to share your products and services with the public. However, while there are certainly tons of people online, the Internet is such a vast marketplace that it will usually take a good deal of marketing to get any real results. Your best retail outlet while just getting started may actually be a local community marketplace. Most metropolitan areas are going to play host to a bevy of swap meets, flea markets, and farmer's markets that can provide great foot-traffic at a bargain rate.

Let's say that your new business sells and installs home windows. This would seem like an unorthodox thing to sell at a venue like a farmer's market, but it's not about the venue, it's about the exposure. Even people buying organic fruits and vegetables are going to need windows for their home at some point. Taking the Orange County Marketplace (a local swap meet in Southern California) for example, space is available for as low as about $60 a day, and they steadily get the foot traffic of tens of thousands of local consumers every weekend. These sorts of venues can be great options starting out, as they are low cost and high exposure. They also usually won't require you to sign any leases or make any other sort of long-term financial commitments.

Another option that will generally cost a little more, is to get a vendor table or booth at an event your target consumers would likely attend. For example, if you were in the business of selling trendy t-shirts aimed towards teens and young adults, it might be lucrative to get a vendor table at a small local music festival for a few hundred dollars.

For businesses that sell to other businesses, local marketplaces aren't obviously as feasible an option, but there are other ways to get in front of potential clients other than the dreaded time-honored techniques of cold calling and going door-to-door. It would be a good idea, for example, to start by getting signed up on LinkedIn (http://www.linkedin.com) if you aren't already a member. Then join any local groups available to business professionals in your area. These groups are likely going to hold semi-regular meetings or mixers where you'll be able to network and share information about your business with other business professionals. You might also consider joining your city's chamber of commerce, which will also undoubtedly hold regular mixers providing the chance to network with yet more business owners in your area.

You can also be advertising your products and/or services online, utilizing free online classified sites such as Craigslist (http://www.craigslist.org). Budget minded small business owners often check these sorts of sites looking for a good deal. There's also usually no reason not to link your company in you 'signature' when posting in online forums and message boards related to your industry, as long as it is done with tact, and doesn't look out of place. You should also of course be giving yourself a plug here and there to your friends and family on any social media platforms that you may also be a part of (Facebook, Twitter, Instagram, etc.). Again I'll reiterate, when advertising through your signature on message boards, or through social media to your friends and family, you always want to make sure you are doing so tastefully, and not in a fashion that makes it look like you are blatantly advertising. You'll also want to make sure that you aren't violating the terms of service of whatever website you are advertising on.

The key with any of these methods, and in fact any form of marketing, is repetition. It's simply unrealistic to assume your sales are just going to take off the second you put your business in the public eye. Let's take the window sales & installation company mentioned earlier for example. If they pop a booth up at the swap meet it's highly unlikely they're going to be selling windows like hot cakes right off the bat, even if they were offering the lowest priced specials on windows that anyone has ever seen. The thing is that for the most part, people are only going to purchase new windows when they actually need new windows. However by standing in front of people and sharing information on their company on a regular and consistent basis, when the time comes that these same people do need new windows, or when someone they know mentions they need new windows, your business will spring to mind.

You probably hear ads for mattress stores and car dealerships on the radio all the time. They don't expect to make a bunch of sales based on any one individual commercial play. They instead are expecting that if they play their ads regularly and constantly enough, that radio listeners will think of them first when they eventually do need a new mattress or car. In much the same way, you'll need to be persistent, and patient, when using whatever method of selling or advertising that you intend to try.

The Budget Entrepreneur

Chapter 9
Time to Grow!

Over the course of this book we've evaluated all the major steps necessary in getting a business off the ground on a tight budget, from conception to making the first sale. If you've followed along you're business is now officially a start-up, and with any luck you'll soon be on your way to making the money needed to take your business to the next level. But what exactly might that entail?

Once you're profitable, and steadily putting money in the bank, you're going to want to protect it. This would be a good time to take a look at turning your sole-proprietorship into a corporation, if you're one of the 70% of small businesses who started off in that business structure. This is easily done, as mentioned earlier in the book, and you won't have to change any of your advertising, or your name and logo, as you can easily and simply transfer your existing fictitious business name to the new corporation. So if you had already established yourself as 'A+ Window Service', this would allow continuing use of that name instead of the new corporations legal name (likely 'A+ Window Service, Inc.' in this instance).

Restructuring your business entity in this fashion will allow you some protection against personal liability should any issues arise now that the company is growing and generating higher sales volume. Remember, the time for counting pennies is behind you; you're making money now and you're going to need to start spending some of it to secure your business's future. Now more than ever is the time to be sure you are consulting with tax and legal professionals to make sure that your business is structured to provide you with the maximum liability protection and tax benefit possible.

You're also probably going to be ready to start looking at dedicated retail or commercial space for your business. Be sure to take your time and search through both newspapers and online classifieds in your area. You should also take a drive through the areas that interest you. A lot of times by driving around you can find amazing deals on space that is being leased by the property owner directly and/or otherwise is not being widely listed as being available for rent or lease through the usual channels.

Finally, it's time to take your marketing to the next level. This is really the topic for another book, but in general just remember the power of repetition. There's absolutely no use in doing one mailer, one radio spot, or one magazine or print ad. The only way you're going to succeed in these or any other type of marketing is by continually putting your information in front of the consumer. This is going to cost money, which is why we haven't touched on this until now. If you want to continue to grow, however, you're going to need to expand your reach. The way to do that is to keep putting yourself in front of your target audience as often as you can afford. When you're ready to spend the money on these types of advertising campaigns, commit a modest budget to the campaign, and be patient. Give yourself no less than thirteen weeks in regard to radio and daily/weekly publications, to six months in regard to magazine and print ads, before you evaluate any given campaign to see if it is beginning to yield positive results.

That just about covers it, so go out there and make some money!

www.ingramcontent.com/pod-product-compliance
Lightning Source LLC
Chambersburg PA
CBHW032019190326
41520CB00007B/548